The Sunshine Project

The Sunshine Project

Ecclesiastes 11:7-8

Francesca Petrino

Published by Tablo

Copyright © Francesca Petrino 2019.
Published in 2019 by Tablo Publishing.

All rights reserved.

This book or any portion thereof may not be reproduced or used in any manner whatsoever without the express written permission of the author except for the use of brief quotations in a book review.

for the broken hearted

rain
grow
blossom

rain

you must need back story
my name is francesca alliene petrino
my soul has longed
for love and music
and all
that i receive
is heartbreak and silence

it stings like a thousand needles
through my skin
as your name
exits my lips

                -the memory of you is worse than any shot

and all of the sudden
i feel really really small
and i hear lots of sounds
and im drowning
in the deep sea
of my surroundings
i have had this feeling
since i was so little

                                                        -i must not be the only one

this is my biggest risk
you are holding me
who i am
everything i have felt
i risk the ways you will interpret me
criticize and assume my past
which is stained into these very pages
you are holding me
take care of me

-or close the damn book

even after months
i can still feel you pulling me closer
and playing with my hair
as you laugh and tell me
how deeply in love you are

-they lied
when they said
i would eventually forget

my mother told me i was unhappy
and i begged myself not to let go
holding onto the days
i used to gush to her
about your kind heart
and then i cried to her
as the same heart
kicked me to the curb

i miss you
not at night
as i look at the stars
or when i am lonely
but in the middle of the day
when my mind grows tired
and i forget
that i am working
on never thinking of you again

the less you think of him
the more you will forget

    -i keep telling myself
    i dont remember
    but then all of a sudden
    someone reminds me of you
    and i realize i still know all those poems
    like the back of my hand

so many girls
have wondered too often
what they do so wrong
to deserve a boy
leaving them with a dying garden
and no rain clouds

you need to love someone new
to show me
that there is no guilt
in starting over

-you go first

weeping willow tree
where shall i be
laying beneath
the cradle of your leaves
protected from all
with your love
weeping willow tree
where shall i be

-i miss the willow tree
that used to live
down the street

i am sorry to say
that sometimes it is the ones who are closest
who end up hurting us the most
by never being as close
as we think they are

-our illusions
of who we think they are
kills us

you do not know
what you are looking for
why come to me
and chase me
when you dont
even know who you are

-please just leave me on my own

i say to her
tell me why you love him

she was quiet
and then she told me
i do not love him

-darling
he cannot be
who you keep asking him to be

if at any point
you find yourself apologizing
for pulling away from him
please just leave him behind

-it is not your fault
you did not do
what you didnt want to do

who is it
that causes your nightmares
is it the same person
whom you greet every morning

-let go

you have no right to insult me
when you have no idea
who i am
or what i have been through

-my new self knows
that i should have left sooner

you lied to me
you knew the lyrics to my songs
and the name of this book
before anyone else
and all you did was lie
as i gave you every special piece of me

                                          -as you read this book
                                 know the reason i succeeded
                                  was because you broke me
                                             and i flourished

you didnt want to stay
no one ever does
but at least this time
he left before i fell in love

he says
i have never been a fan
of black nail polish
you know
it is quite funny
i have never been a fan
of any of your opinions

sometimes i wonder what she goes through
look in her eyes
how hurt she is
i try to talk to her
she doesnt hold onto anyone
not anymore

                              -i cant save her alone

it is my job
i am supposed to protect you
you say
i love you
on the phone
as you hold the gun to your soul
and ask permission
from me
to pull the trigger

                        -good friends who make bad decisions

you don't notice
the wounds you open
of others
until they are bleeding
all over you

-selfish

she is trying to laugh more
she is trying to smile brighter
she is trying to be kind
it breaks my heart
i know her too well
to believe
that she is really happy

                              -her smile is wide
                              but her eyes are sad

you burn your lungs away
and you talk in horrible ways
of the people who try to love you
everyone is drowning in their feelings
while also
trying to seem
like they dont care at all

                              -no one knows
                               what they
                               are doing

you force your heart to beat
for all the wrong reasons
and all the wrong people

-when your heart sinks to the floor
every time he speaks
you dont love him

i refuse to believe
that if you wanted to be with me
you just would
maybe that desire is not enough

-how do I wait
never knowing
if you will come around
as I always do for you

i am the novel
the one you borrow dozens of times
you photograph
the poems
on my worn
ripped pages
you highlight
your favorite parts
yet
you never keep me
i am always returned
tattered and worn
wondering the next time
you will check me out

-you love everything
enough to keep coming back
but not enough to stay

get out
you do not belong
get out
i pray to God
take them away

-when the voices are all loud
i do not know
which one
is me speaking

letting my guard down
is so easy
i hate myself for it
every time i fall
they leave
yet i still fall
and end up having to pick myself up
no one
ever
helps
me
stand

-please

sometimes
good people
make bad choices
and bad people
make good choices
it does not
mean they have changed

 -you wear a mask

you say
you are here
if i need anything at all
i sob to my pillow
and my heart becomes so heavy
and you
are nowhere to be found

-your 32nd lie
was that youd be there for me
even after youre gone

who were you
before this world
stripped you of your clothes
and dressed you back up
in all of the colors you despise

when people ask
what a panic attack feels like
i tell them
when you skip a step on the stairs
and your heart drops for half a second
it is like
that half a second
is dragged on
until i am on the floor
gasping for air
and i can feel the tears dripping off my chin

-it feels like dying

who are you
i do not recognize you
or your decisions
or the things you say
how did i ever defend you
maybe
maybe because of your past
and what you have been through
your poor soul has been so hurt
that your heart turned cold
who are you
i do not recognize you

-you are a rainstorm that goes on for days

do you know how many times
they look at me
at the clothes on my body
or the shoes on my feet
and they laugh
at the pure sight of me

                                              -what about me
                                                    is so funny
                  that you truly cannot wait until im not around
                                        to laugh about me

he shoots you down
over and over and over again
and you pick yourself up
every single time
you cover your bullet holes with a cloth
and run into his arms
as he pulls you by your hair
and shoves you through the door

-stop accepting his apologies

i am giving myself to you
in a slow drip
in pieces
i reveal myself
the problem is
as soon as i give pieces
someone leaves
right in the middle of me

-i am a puzzle
and people keep taking my pieces
and losing them

i have this small hope
that you are still thinking of me
but it is the worst in people
and especially in you
that they do not remember the hurt they caused
if they were never around to see it

i am so lost in myself
i try to believe any reason
for someone not to stay
besides that it is me

-maybe it is always me

you cannot
force someone
to open up to you
they will share what they want to share

-do not scrape
every bit of secret
they have within them

grow

there will be great trouble in the world
-mt 24 1:28

overthinking will destroy your mood
breathe and let go
your mind cannot let go
if you keep forcing it
into the wrong mindset
stop checking your phone
stop asking questions you dont want the answers to
stop wondering what other people think

-the first step of growing is looking within

you do not speak to me
you do not check in
you do not look at me
or ask my friends how i am
i guess i need to understand
everything you are spelling out for me
you do not miss me
i should not go after you
because you
are not running after me

-we are playing tug of war
and you are giving no energy
my hands are weak and blistered
pulling and pulling for you
until i reach the end of the rope
and realize
i have been begging for someone
who isnt even here

he says he loves me
just because he wants
for me to write about him
well
my darling
here is your poem
wish granted

-you lied
just to know what it feels like
to experience actual love
and you proved me right
that you are heartless

we show off our lost loves
we parade them on our arms
with the photos not deleted
the letters still in our pockets
and we walk around
with frowns
and watch our careless hearts
dragging behind us on the floor

you dont miss him
you miss the joy
your heart held
when he was there

-your smiles relied on him
and now your eyes have to learn
how to light up
without seeing him

how do you miss someone
who was hardly ever there

                        -you fell in love with the absence
                                they transformed into
                            and it was okay for a while
                                        because even
                         when they were not around
                              they still were yours

the night
that we looked at the sky
i should have taken it
as a sign
that there was not one star

-starless skies are what terrify me the most

we were so confused
we killed each other
and called it love
but we were like drugs
good while it lasted
but painful
the second it left our lungs

    -even when you are sober
    your heart may still hurt
    at the sight of him

i apologize
i know i hurt you too
each day
at the end of it all
i screamed
how nothing was my fault
i was wrong
i am sorry
it took so long
for me to realize
you are not the only one to blame

                    -we were both clueless about love
                        and tried to teach each other

if i don't miss you anymore
does that mean
it was never real

-i suppose ill never know
and that is fine
because i dont think
i want to know

i find myself apologizing to him
for everything i do
but he reassures me every time
this new love of mine

                                          -even if he does not stay
                                                he has taught me
                                       love should not be fearful

after my heart is broken
i search everywhere
for the missing pieces
and so often
i pick up the wrong ones
and end up running
after someone
i do not even want

-i did to you what i swore i would never do

you said we would dance
did you dance?
as you walked away
from the little bit
we had built

why is it
that i always feel so free
when someone leaves
yet i still miss them

-the relief
is like a breath of fresh air
until i remember
you are gone

i wrote in the sand
my dream for you and me
only for a wave
to wash it away at my feet

you do not know
how bad a storm is
until it passes
and you are left
alone
picking up the damage

 -i wonder how long it takes to feel whole after love leaves

do not compare the ones
capable to love you
to the one
you did not love correctly in the first place

how is it
that when everything is good
the smallest mishaps
are the ones that break us
i lay here
trying so hard to be happy
yet i am crying in your arms

-healing is not consistent

it is on the nights
when everything is well
and in place
that i wish you would come back
to see so much joy

you brought me so much joy
but you took it with you
and now i am left
to make my own

-i will have to learn
to create the sunshine
instead of depending on you for it

i find it sad
that there are so many damaged souls
who do not know better
so they treat kindness
like a privilege

-you deserve more

i have so much sunshine to give
no one ever wants to stay
but it is okay
i must learn to keep my happiness
to myself
rather than give
to those who dont deserve it

i will never learn
to take my own advice
i will never learn
to read these poems
as letters
and consider them
addressed to me

he is my greatest love i tell you
i cry to him in the night
as my heart breaks
and he stays up every time
sewing my broken pieces together

-this is what safety feels like

i feel bad for God
we so often hate
and hurt ourselves
and each other
all of his creations
everything he has made
we criticize
and tear down
and scold
but why?

-if we love the creator
why do we hate the creations?

you are amazing
that is what he tells me
the only things that are amazing in this world
are the sun and the stars

-i am neither

a little girl asked me
why my phone had a notification
that read
please smile
how do i tell her
it is because
i wanted to be happy
and i was not
i am now
yet i will never get rid of the notification
in fear
that it will be defeat
having to get it back
when once again
i become overwhelmed
with sadness

it is when your heart is quiet
that your mind throws tantrums

-listen to yourself

they tell me i have gotten so much better
they say that
because instead of being
who i love
i am who they love

he asks me
why i have never written about the stars
i tell him
that i have seen too many starless skies
to believe in something
so inconsistent
yet so beautiful
that would be
like breaking my own heart

-i only trust the sun

i tell everyone that i am leaving
they laugh
everyone wants to get away
but the problem is
they run with themselves
as they try to escape their own skin
i am no different

no one has ever called me angel
probably because
no part of me
is safe from the cruelty
that society has buried into my mind

                              -instead of letting people
                                    teach us about hate
                                  why dont we teach them
                                            about love

she says i was the first to tell her the truth of love
the more you love
the more memories you make
the more it will hurt
as you watch their eyes drift
to someone else
and you are left alone
with your heart in your hands

-a lesson i learned in the hardest three months of my life

i want to live
in the loudest way possible
with my hair always down
and a smile plastered on my face
and my nails painted all different colors

he slips his hands
around the lining of my face
and i am scared
because it feels right
it feels so right
to start to love him

-this is the beginning again
and i am ready

i carried him to the middle of the sky
and i pointed at clouds i loved
and i sang to him the songs i grew up with
and i think
that i had to teach someone else to love me
so that i would love me
and instead of falling for you

    -i fell for me

you wanted me to carry you
to the ends of the earth
but as i began to take you in
you whispered to me
how you didnt like
any of the little things about me

we are all
who we swore
we would never be

                              -and the little girl
                            that lives inside me
                         would be so dissapointed
                               if she only knew
                             how i let you treat me

she is mean
i know
only because she was raised
in a place
where the love was so faint
she does not know better
than to love in a way
that feels like hate and happiness
all at the same time

kindness
is what your mother calls you
even on her hardest days

-little girl

i wear what i like
and they tell me how they feel
and then i wear
what they like

                    -if it is my body
                 then why do i let them
               decide what i would like
                   to dress her up with

look at the mascara
that drips from your eyes onto your hands
and all of the pain it resembles
but also
all that you have been through
and you are still standing

                         -even if you are stained with the deep black
                                  that covers your eyes
                                        you are still here
                                    and that is enough

i do not think you are coming back
and somehow
i finally feel okay

                      -because even after you are gone
                  when i stand in front of the world
                      i still see the flowers dancing
                     and i still feel wind on my face
               which means even after you are gone
                   the world has not stopped turning

everyone leaves
and i am understanding
to not trust anyone
but myself

                                              -i will never leave my side

think about who
you would love
to love

what scares me
is that sometimes it rains
but a rainbow never follows
we are left at the bottom of the world
awaiting beauty
only to be looking at an empty sky
but maybe
the emptiness is more beautiful
than any sky filled with color
because then
we cannot help but notice
everything else
that we have to be happy about

blossom

freckles splatter and bloom
like paint and petals in the spring
and fade like memories and watercolor
in the deepest thoughts of winter

-you are as beautiful as the earth

loves
like snowmen
we build them up
with everything we can find
and sometimes
they stay for a really long time
but some melt away
leaving pieces still behind
but all of the good love
stays around
to visit now and then
whether it is next winter
or just in photographs

thank you
for taking care of yourself
before me
thank you
for being the first
to handle my heart responsibly
and letting go
when you knew
there was not anything left
to hold on to

                      -honesty hurts but im so glad you told me

sometimes
great people come
and great people leave
you cannot be mad
they did nothing wrong
you just have to accept it
and be thankful
for the joy
they brought in the time
that they were still here

                    -and as i used to read the poems
                         i wrote when i was in love
                              i would cry and cry
                                          but now
                                 now i am so joyful
                                      and thankful
                   that i experienced something so real

they can take everything from you
they can take everyone from you
but they cannot ever take
the sun
that you see every day
only the moon
and God
can do such a task

sometimes
i look at myself
and i do not recognize a thing
yet
i am beginning to think
this is not
so bad

-maybe this is what growing feels like

it must hurt
and i apologize
to all of the people who let me go
because i am the sunshine
the light that they search for
in everyone else
but it is only me

-does it hurt to see me with all this joy
i know you thought
you drowned me
by leaving
but oh darling
thats what saved me

i hope sunshine reminds you of me
every time you step outside
and soft songs you fall asleep to
and poetry that runs
off of the tip of your tongue
and in the nights you can't sleep
you crave me
but you let me go
like a dandelion in the wind
i will be forced
to drift away
from who would not have me stay

upon the ones
whom you have made suffer
wish new beginnings and healing
as you smile in their direction

and when the new beginning comes
and gets rough

do not mistake his mistakes
for ruin
you make mistakes as well
do not define each other
by every mess up
but more by every time
you flourish

-forward

life is too short
to wonder
if you are ready
to be happy again

-leap into the next chapter of your life
with open eyes
and an open mind

as you read
please smile
and i will be fulfilled

-even if i am the only one who reads
and even if i am the only one who smiles

you read the words i wrote
on tear stained pages
in the nights of my years
that i fell in and out of love with boys
and fell in love with myself

her toes sink in the sand
as she sinks into you
with every breath
the salty air gets in her lungs
she breathes into you
but she is the only one who drowns

-do not make her fall for you
if you are not planning
to hold her hands
as she tries
to stay afloat in the waves

thank the ones who leave
for teaching you what you should value
and how you should be treated
and how to treat the next
then
you thank yourself
for forgiving
there is no more battle to fight

                                                        -rest

kindness
kindness is what shows you
all of the layers to a person

        -maybe you do not know much about them
        because you never bothered to smile at them

you have to live
live for the paintings
with color dripping from the sides
live for the nights you cannot stop laughing
and for the days
you look at yourself
and your heart is so full
that you find everything you see
in the mirror
beautiful

think of the people
who are always
nothing but kind to you
spend more time with them

                        -your happiness is staring you in the face
                              waiting for you to take her in

they weep
and lay low
filled with color
overflowing at the seams
the saddest
and most beautiful
of them all

                                                -weeping willows
                                                        are proof
                                        you can hurt and grow
                                            at the same time

she writes her poems
all over your skin
and when you kick her out of your bed
you still sing the words
as a melody
in your sleep

> -you miss her but she deserves better
> than someone who reads the poems
> but will never understand them

luck is on my side
reads the charm on my bracelet

        -i aspire the day i will feel happy and lucky
                without a reminder
                    that i should be

do not let others decide
how long
you need
to move on from someone

-take as much
or as little time
as you need
to heal

sometimes
God puts you in hands you do not belong in
so those people
will know the hurt
of losing sunshine
and you will know the relief
of losing darkness

-i love this book

people are colors
and my sweet friends
tell me i am a yellow person
this is my favorite compliment
but remember that
sunshine always goes away
when the moon takes over

                        -yellow people cannot always be happy

there is no sunset
without sunrise
you must rise to fall
you must fall to rise

                                                    -changes come in time

i guess
it has been you
this whole time

                    -all i had to do was extend my hand
                  because you have always been ready

hopelessly drowning
in the deep blue
that is you

                                  -if this is what drowning feels like
                                then i want to feel it for the rest of my life

the broken index of your favorite book
the song your mother sang
as you opened your eyes in the morning
a canvas filled with more color
than the most beautiful sunset you have ever seen
eyes full of joy and grace

                                        -falling for him
                                          will feel like
                        each of your favorite feelings
                                            all at once

this year
i will draw myself
with more
than just one color

-i am so tired of painting for everyone else

what do you two even talk about
is what they ask me

well
we talk of sunsets
and oceans
and skies
and colors
and on the nights i cannot sleep
he sings to me

-you think i am lying
for the poetry
but i am not

i guess i was not enough
but the joke
is on you
i never asked to be enough for you
i am for me

                                                -and after all this time
                                                i finally feel whole again

at times
i feel as though
i am the only one kind to me
but i am so proud of myself
you see
i have evolved so that
i am perfectly content
in being my own best friend

i hope you smile again
and when you do
you remember the source
of your joy

			-make your happiness consistent

never feel guilty
for being vulnerable to the ones you love
you are in the midst of this world
falling for so many
taking so many chances
thank yourself
for living so purely

-love as many people as you can
and as often as you can

your mistakes
do not define your soul
only what you choose to do
how you heal
and how you treat everyone you meet
defines you
breathe
move forward

-you have to forgive yourslef

they romanticize the ocean blue eyes
and I always thought mine were okay
brown eyes
and i know they arent the sea
and i know they arent the sky
but i love them so much
golden golden golden

-please fall in love
with my eyes
before anything

live for yourself
and your sweet eyes
live and strive to bring smiles
not only to others
but to yourself as well

-it is okay to put yourself first

gift yourself
with simple kindness
tell yourself you look beautiful
and that you love you
that you will make time for yourself
and if you need anything at all
be there

                                            -be your own soul mate first

i set reminders
dinging throughout the day
telling me
to smile
be kind
keep my head up
and look where i am now

                                                    -train yourself

hills
over and over
consistency
is what i crave
with everything and everyone

                        -if you say you love me today
                              will you love me
                                  in a million seconds

how kind
that a boy
compares me
to the greatest star of them all
the one i find the most joy in

-hello sunshine

you are beautiful
because of everything you are
and everything you are not

                    -God put so much time and thought
                                  into creating you

he calls me sunshine
i never like to rhyme
but oh my God
he is the light
that frees my heart from my mind
so take me
in your arms
i am your sunshine

                                        -i meant for this to be a song

you will know you love him
by sunsets
and even more by sunrises
because they are so breathtaking
your mind wanders off
to whom you love most
and all of the sudden
you are looking at beauty
and thinking of it as well

                                                -love is blind
                                                       is a lie
                            love makes me see the world
                                          as a globe
                                  exploding at the seams
                                        with beauty

i thank God
every
single
day
for taking you away from me

-how funny to think
i once begged him
to send you back

little girl
come look at this world
beneath your feet
every mountain and wave
waiting for your eyes
to get lost in them

poetry
makes my soul beg
for an adventurous youth
and a joyful adulthood

i hope that if i ever go blind
it is due to always staring
at the most beautiful sun
i have ever seen

if you ever feel unwanted
because you are too happy
for everyone around you to handle
just think
that no one looks at the sun
because it is always too bright

                              -but what would we do without her

when you pour me hot chocolate
and run your fingers
through my auburn hair
is when i will fall in love

i wish we danced like we used to
i would love to be swept off my feet
dipped and held gently
twirled at the hand of a boy
only looking at me

-he taught me to dance
in my kitchen
on a tuesday afternoon
as the sun shined

it is almost as if God has my soul in his hands
on some days
i can feel him guiding me
because when i cry
my cat sleeps with me
on the days i wake up hopeless
the sun shines bright
begging me to come out
from beneath my sheets
and on the wonderful days
he sends my mother to laugh with me
and on the nights i am not sure who i am
he sits and holds my hand
as my mind wraps around itself
for me to write words like these

-i know he is with me

no one knows
where they will be tomorrow
love everyone
as if you won't ever be able to love them
after today

dont settle for cloudy skies

i wake up
every day
to a painting that reads
"do more than exist"

-i love to live
with love in my soul

i am beautiful
please say it
like you are speaking
to your best friend when she cries to you
say it like you are speaking to your mother
say it to yourself
with the same love and tone
you use as you speak to others

she stands with the broken pieces
that were once her heart
and she weaves them together
with the needle and thread
that the moon has handed her

treat yourself gently
like you are holding the hand
of the boy you love
or like guiding a baby
as they walk across the grass of a backyard for the first time
treat yourself
like your entire life
is your greatest accomplishment

                        -you have to take care of yourself
                    like the sun takes care of the sunflowers

look at yourself
like you look at the flowers you see
on the side of the road
as the sun comes in
on your way to school

                                                      -love this world
                                    and it will love you back

once you notice the beautiful things
in everyone you love
you will notice the beautiful things
in yourself as well
and you will love you
just as i love you

she says no one cares
little does she know
everyone loves
and cares
more than she will ever see

-i promise
you are more noticeable
than you believe

smile
at everyone around you
all on their own journey
all struggling
yet blooming at the same time

-we are all daisies in a downpour

i look at everyone around me
differently now
they all smile
at such wonderful things
i love my friends

-the sun must weep
when she has to be apart
from them in the night

she cries to me on the phone
"he doesn't listen
he doesn't care
he hates me now
he yells at me"
i tell her to leave
she responds with
"Francesca, he loves me"

                                          -maybe
                                    unhealthy love
                                         is blind

when you fall off your bike
because you forgot to balance
and you just went for it
you never trusted yourself
with so much control
ever again
that is why
we never love as much
as we loved our first

she asks me what love feels like
my mind begged my heart
to tell her to run the other way
and not believe in such foolish things
but then my soul
led my lips
as i explained
what every waking moment feels like
when you are in love

he grows roots in me
as he makes me believe
in a thing called
love

-he is painting my soul
all of his favorite colors

i wonder when the time will come
that i will tell him
of all the love
i have been saving for him

        -our first i love you cannot come fast enough

the sun smiles
when the flowers bloom
and God does the same
for me and you

i said how did we get here
he said
i have always loved you

god smiles
when you tell yourself
how wonderfully beautiful you are
more so
than when a boy tells you

-he loves when they are kind to you
but he loves it more
when they dont have to be
because you are already content

i lay on my soft sheets
the rain is in puddles
the stars and moon
have already waved goodbye
it smells like honeysuckle
my heart flutters
as she can see the light
even if the sun is hidden
beneath the weight of the clouds

god smiles at you
when you wake up
to the sunshine

                                                  -welcome home i love you

about the author

Francesca Petrino is currently a junior at The Heritage School in Newnan, Georgia. She has always loved writing. Even as a toddler, she would have her mom staple papers together so she could make books. This is her first published book, and she is so happy to share it with readers around the world. She also enjoys performing in musicals with multiple companies. She would like to thank you for supporting her in her dream.

Lightning Source UK Ltd.
Milton Keynes UK
UKHW041418150419
341050UK00002B/846/P